Without You!

By the same author

Poetry Introduction 7
Faber and Faber

Steel Horizon: North Sea Poems
Incline Press

Ordinary Others
Drizzle-Dazzle

Vulgar Variants
Drizzle-Dazzle

The Lady on the Plank: Poems for Ukraine
Drizzle-Dazzle

Until Independence Day: More Poems for Ukraine
Drizzle-Dazzle

JONATHAN WONHAM

Without You!

POEMS FOR UKRAINE 3

With illustrations by
NICK WONHAM

Drizzle - Dazzle

First published in 2023
by Drizzle-Dazzle

Poems © Jonathan Wonham 2023
www.jonathanwonham.com

Illustrations © Nick Wonham 2023

ISBN 978-1-8382880-8-2

Typeset at www.szcz.uk

Printed and bound by 4edge Limited, UK

Dedicated to the memory of three courageous volunteers, Andrew Bagshaw, Chris Parry and Pete Reed, killed in the first months of 2023.

All three came to Ukraine to offer assistance as humanitarian aid workers and all three were active at the frontline in the east of the country, evacuating Ukrainian citizens from around the Bakhmut and Soledar area. Despite travelling in civilian vehicles, they were targeted by Russian weapons close to the frontline.

.

Do you still think that we are 'one nation?' Do you still think that you can scare us, break us, make us make concessions? You really did not understand anything? Don't understand who we are? What are we for? What are we talking about?

Read my lips: Without gas or without you? Without you. Without light or without you? Without you. Without water or without you? Without you. Without food or without you? Without you. Cold, hunger, darkness and thirst are not as scary and deadly for us as your 'friendship and brotherhood'. But history will put everything in its place. And we will be with gas, light, water and food… and WITHOUT you!'

PRESIDENT ZELENSKYY, 12 SEPTEMBER 2022

We are waging a war against a country 28 times the size of our country, with a population four times larger than ours, a country whose military potential is many times greater than ours. We are waging a war on land, in the air, at sea and in cyberspace. We've been waging a war not for eight months, but for eight years and eight months. All this testifies to our resilience, the courage to defend what is ours and the thirst to win.

VALERIY ZALUZHNYI, COMMANDER-IN-CHIEF OF UAF, 31 OCTOBER 2022

I want to say to everyone in Russia – and from Russia – who still hasn't been able to say even a few words condemning this terrorism, despite seeing and knowing everything perfectly well. Your cowardly silence, your attempt to 'wait out' the things that are happening, will only end with these same terrorists coming for you, too, one day. Evil is very sensitive to cowardice. Evil always remembers those who fear it or who try to bargain with it. And when it comes for you, there will be no one to protect you.

PRESIDENT ZELENSKYY, 15 JANUARY 2023

If you pretend that [fascism] is merely an aberration which will presently pass off of its own accord, you are dreaming a dream from which you will awake when somebody coshes you with a rubber truncheon.

GEORGE ORWELL, *THE ROAD TO WIGAN PIER* (1937)

CONTENTS

PREFACE

This is the third book of poems I have written about the Russian invasion of Ukraine. The first two books sold out quickly and between them raised £2,758 for Ukrainian refugees. Immersing myself in the news of the war for a year has not been easy, but has always seemed very necessary. I felt adamant from Day 1 of the 2022 invasion that Russia's actions were wrong and deeply malign, and nothing has persuaded me since that anyone should have the slightest flicker of sympathy for that country's aims. Indeed, the longer the war continues, the more I (and most of the world) realise how evil the regime is and how deeply state TV propaganda has affected the views of ordinary Russians towards their Ukrainian neighbours. It is Russia's sense of superiority over Ukraine that has allowed this war to occur. This sentiment seems based on a denial of Ukraine's culture and long history together with renewed imperialist chutzpah.

Russia is not a homogeneous entity. There are undoubtedly many people in Russia who resist the Putin regime and what is happening in Ukraine, but there is also a counter-movement of people who are becoming persuaded by the government's actions. Since the invasion, Russia's internal security forces have expended a great deal of energy cracking down on dissent, ensuring that those who speak out lose their jobs or leave the country through fear. This effect has been well documented for the theatre industry in Russia by a long article in the *FT Magazine*, which speaks about 'zigateatry', the process by which theatres all over Russia have begun displaying large 'Z' symbols on their facades to show their obeisance to the regime. Imagine the fear and pressure such moves put on individuals working in theatres who feel they should protest. According to the article, theatres in Russia are well attended, but they have become places where only comedy and jokes are allowed, and the jokes are usually cruel ones.

My previous book *Until Independence Day* covered the sixth month of the war (July–August 2022) and ended with the news of a major Ukrainian counter-offensive in the Kharkiv region of north-east Ukraine. This successful military operation pushed back Russian defences over a very large area which has since been held by Ukraine. Within that territory lay Izyum. This town, invaded in April, was used by Russia as a key military hub to supply its forces from the east. In mid-September, excavations began of makeshift graves in a forest close by. Some of the graves contained more than one body and the first to be excavated revealed a woman who had a rope around her neck. According to Ukrainian investigators, 447 bodies were discovered, including 414 bodies of civilians (215 men, 194 women, 5 children) and 22 servicemen. Most of the dead showed signs of violent death and 30 presented traces of torture and summary execution.

In the autumn of 2022, a new phase of the war began when, in the early morning of 8 October, a fire broke out on the vast Kerch Strait Bridge as a result of an explosion. The bridge, which connects Russia to Crimea, was built by Russia after it occupied the Ukrainian territory of Crimea in 2014. The explosion damaged both the road carriageway and the railway line above it. In supposed retaliation for this event, the next day Russia began using long-range missiles to target sites all over Ukraine. The missiles have been mainly aimed at infrastructure in the energy and water sectors in an attempt to destroy the whole population's access to electricity, gas and fresh water.

The Kerch Strait Bridge was a major supply route to Crimea and the south of Ukraine, and with its destruction a second major Ukrainian offensive could begin in the south to take back lands on the west of the Dnipro including, on 11 November, the city of Kherson. The Kherson liberation was a joyful event for the people who lived there, but revealed more horrors of Russian war crimes: evidence of torture and extrajudicial killings. Departing from Kherson, Russian forces removed art and historical objects from the Oleksii Shovkunenko Art Museum using unmarked trucks. During the war, Russia has destroyed or damaged over 30 Ukrainian museums and over 500 cultural institutions, and has stolen almost 15,000 pieces of art from the Kherson region alone. Experts say it is the biggest art heist since the Nazis' plundering in the Second World War. Even the bones of Catherine the Great's lover, Grigory Potemkin, have been dug up from a crypt in St Catherine's Cathedral and made off with.

Russia's cruel policy of targeting civilian infrastructure has not been effective: utility networks have been repaired and Ukrainians remain staunchly resistant to the Russian occupation despite winter temperatures as low as −20°C. Meanwhile, most of the EU has been having a relatively mild winter, a benefit given the interruption of Russian gas exports to Europe and another failure in Russia's attempt to bully the world. On 14 January 2023, the day this book begins, Russia launched its tenth wave of long-range missile strikes at Ukraine, attempting to destroy infrastructure and weaken Ukrainian resistance. I had not intended to start writing this third instalment of poems until 24 January, but a devastating attack on an apartment in Dnipro by a Russian missile provoked me to begin.

17 March 2023

In the Yellow Kitchen

Are the chairs still standing
with their backs to the wall
that isn't there?

Are the children's benches
still stowed under the table
quite safely?

Do those apples always
remain piled in their basket
like a still life
frozen to the core?

And did anyone brave
the damaged stairs
to remove the microwave oven
or the television set
hung above it?

How did the news come so quickly
that the walls were immediately opened up
to reveal a landscape from *Inferno*?

And how did he suddenly become part of it,
the father who is now deceased –

who put his children to bed,
read them stories, told them
everything will be OK?

Bad Dream

How to heal the burns
a civilian has received
from phosphorous attack?

Go inside them and writhe
like a snake shedding its skin.
Writhe till you wake up.

The UK has become the first Western power to offer to supply Ukraine with main battle tanks. Prime Minister Rishi Sunak has confirmed the UK will provide fourteen Challenger 2 tanks and other advanced artillery support in the coming weeks. The pledge was made this morning during a call with President Zelenskyy as a sign of the UK's ambition to intensify support to Ukraine. This decision will pile further pressure on Germany to approve a delivery of German Leopard tanks. Russia carried out two mass rocket attacks on Ukraine today. Ukrainian authorities said the targets were the country's energy infrastructure; however, one rocket devastated an occupied apartment block in Dnipro. Rescue efforts in the ruins of the apartment continued until the following Tuesday when they were finally called off. At that time, the official death toll was 46 with 11 people still missing and a further 80 people injured. Also today, former Russian President Dmitry Medvedev accused the Japanese Prime Minister, Fumio Kishida, of shameful subservience to the US and suggested he should ritually disembowel himself. The EU is planning its tenth package of economic sanctions against Russia, intending to damage the economy and Russia's ability to continue pursuing its invasion of Ukraine.

Mobiks

Ministers of the Russian Federation
call on remote workers grafting online
to return home immediately
and be drafted into the firing line.

Russian long-range missile strikes on energy infrastructure caused emergency power
outages across 11 regions of Ukraine. The Russian government estimates that 100,000
IT workers, representing 10% of the nation's tech workforce, have left Russia since
the invasion of Ukraine and a 'partial' mobilisation of reserves last year, while some
80,000 IT specialists continue to work for Russian companies from abroad. To
counter this exodus, Russian tech giant VK is demanding its employees based abroad
return to Russia and lawmakers are considering a legal ban on remote work. VK,
which employs more than 10,000 people, owns the popular Mail.ru email and news
services as well as the VKontakte and Odnoklassniki social networks. VK CEO
Vladimir Kirienko is the son of Sergei Kirienko, the deputy head of President
Vladimir Putin's administration. In June 2022, it was reported that President Putin
had made Sergei Kirienko responsible for the self-proclaimed 'people's republic' in
Donbas as well as other Russian-occupied territories in Ukraine.

Putin Save Us

Putin we send you this video
so that you can see
the trenches we should occupy
at minus 20°C.

They're full of frozen water
only fit for skating there.
Please Putin, try to save us
since no one else cares.

MONDAY 16 JANUARY (DAY 327)
Russia and Belarus have begun joint air force drills triggering fears in Kyiv and the
West that Moscow could use its ally to launch a new ground offensive in Ukraine. It
is reported that Russia's aerospace forces arrived at Belarusian airfields late last night
and that the planned combat training began this morning. Belarus has described the
drills as purely defensive. The country was used as a base for Russian troops to
launch their failed assault on Kyiv in February 2022. German defence minister
Christine Lambrecht today asked Chancellor Olaf Scholz to accept her resignation.
Her decision comes as Germany faces pressure from Western partners to approve an
increase in international military support for Kyiv. Videos have emerged of Russian
troops complaining about conditions at the frontline. One shows Russian mobilised
men (mobiks) from the 392nd Regiment requesting Putin himself to pay attention to
the deplorable state of their defensive positions and the lack of supplies as they try to
break the thick ice in the trench they've been assigned with their machine gun butts.

Seasonal Deaths 2022 (*Part 2*)

July makes all the faces red.
Yuri Voronov, CEO of *Gazprom* subcontractor,
receives a bullet in the head.

August breeze is heaven sent.
Dan Rapoport, former Moscow nightclub owner,
plunges from his apartment.

September swallows up and go.
Ravil Maganov, chairman of *Lukoil* PJSC,
leaves hospital via the window.

October pumpkins at the door.
Nikolai Mushegian, co-founder of *MakerDAO*,
is washed up on the shore.

November storms turn into gales.
Vyacheslav Taran, president of *Libertex* Group,
dies when his helicopter fails.

December snow brings jingle bells.
Pavel Antov, Russian sausage meat tycoon,
falls off the roof of his hotel.

From bud of spring to summer bloom,
from autumn bronze to winter gloom,

the turning year has circled round,
all months and seasons to themselves remaining true
while death finds new ways to confound.

The first part of this poem can be found in my previous book, Until Independence Day.

Observe the Tank

Observe the tank, can run forwards
as fast as in reverse. Seems owned
by one, yet controlled by another
who must always sign off on its use.

Behold the signer, built it for peace,
made so many and controlled them all.
Not for use against friends we hear
but... a turret can turn right round.

TUESDAY 17 JANUARY (DAY 328)
Andriy Yermak, head of the Ukrainian presidential staff, said more than 9,000
civilians, including 453 children, had been killed in Ukraine since Russia's invasion
last February. Speaking at the World Economic Forum in the Swiss resort of Davos,
Yermak added that Ukraine wanted a special international tribunal to try Russian
political leaders and reparations for the destruction caused by Russia's invasion. The
UN said it had confirmed 7,031 civilian deaths but believes actual casualty tolls are
'considerably higher' given the pending corroboration of many reports and the
inaccessibility of areas where intense fighting is taking place. Poland's Prime Minister
Mateusz Morawiecki has said that Germany should take decisive action and send all
sorts of weapons to Ukraine, implicitly criticising the German Chancellor Olaf
Scholz for his reluctance to supply Kyiv with battle tanks.

In War There are No Accidents

In war there are no accidents.

In war there are   accidents.

       there r no accidents.

In war there are no acc   .

In war   no accidents.

In   no accidents.

In war   are no

In war there are no accidents.

   war there

In war there

        In war   there

In war there

In war there   here

In war here   no   war.   no

Mr Lavrov's Final Solution

So, Mr Lavrov, who are you fighting against now?
Is it Nazis or satanists? NATO or the US?
With so many moving targets it must be hellish
just to shoot straight, which explains a lot I guess.
Now you're saying the West 'unleashed a hybrid war'
against Russia, and that's why you invaded Ukraine.
Was this 'war', by chance, the Maidan Revolution
enacted by Ukrainians in hope of change?

You speak of Russia's 'legitimate interest'
to protect the 'ethnic Russians' in Ukraine…
Well, Mr Lavrov, 'ethnic Russians' circle the globe,
will you flatten all their hometowns just the same
as you did in Mariupol, Maryinka, Bakhmut, Soledar?
It seems to me you're like the bully-clown
who, when the other kids won't let him play,
runs out and kicks their new sandcastles down.

You try to convince us that Russia has the right
to 'remove military infrastructure from Ukraine
that poses a direct threat to your country'.
But the way you set about it's quite deranged:
firstly, by freezing old ladies underground
then destroying apartments and entire towns
and, in Ukrainian hospitals, trying to ensure
that life-support machines are all shut down.

For months now, you've been hell-bent to destroy
Ukraine's energy grid, aiming to splinter
that nation's hopes with darkness and cold.
Remorseless attacks in the midst of winter
via missiles fired from the far-off Caspian Sea
that leave the whole sky streaked with contrail marks
as they strike at power plants and transformers
or even the occasional kiddies' play park.

And then you say that the West has 'a final solution'
for Russia. Frankly, it pains me to hear your fascist bleats
artfully confusing the concept of a death camp
with the concept of an aggressor's defeat.
Stand up and face the jury, Mr Lavrov –
they see you are a gilded monster in a suit,
they've seen your soldiers raid Kherson Museum
and drive away like Nazis with the loot.

They've seen civilians murdered in the street,
torture chambers and means of torture all revealed,
hundreds of shallow graves and heartbroken dogs
pawing the ground where their owners were concealed.
It's Russia that's enacted 'a final solution'
by signing up criminals who are sent to Ukraine –
joined up with Wagner and pushed into battle lines
to pay for your vain ambition with mangled brains.

WEDNESDAY 18 JANUARY (DAY 329)
14 people have died due to a helicopter crash at Brovary, a suburb of Kyiv, including
Ukraine's interior minister Denys Monastyrskiy and other senior officials. The
helicopter crashed into the roof of a kindergarten killing all ten occupants together
with one child and three adults on the ground. Twenty-five other people were
injured, including eleven children. Monastyrskiy, who was responsible for the police
and security inside Ukraine, is the most senior Ukrainian official to die since the war
began. The helicopter was travelling in foggy conditions when it came down in an
area with a number of tall buildings. President Zelenskyy has described the crash as
'a terrible tragedy' and a 'black morning'. Speaking at the World Economic Forum in
Davos by remote link, he said, 'In war, there are no accidents.' In Moscow, Mr Lavrov
told a press conference this morning that the West has the same goal as Adolf Hitler,
who presided over the deaths of tens of millions with his 'final solution'.

On the Rooftops

They say that on the rooftops, ghosts dictate
what poets write. On rooftops, our most marvellous
paper houses are set alight, while in the street
the unknown killers go by, or a drunken brawl
evaporates. And as for me? Let's just say
I have a special gift for ledges and chimney pots –
here's where I was born and where I'll shine.
When the surly laughter gets too strong, I'm here
to arc their vicious humour over the gate.

For so many years I've been a shadow, unobserved,
but still I remain, preserver of all complaints.
Sometimes, I set small fires where pigeons
warm their breasts. Sometimes, I sing too loud
and wake your dreams. Of course, I was there
on the day of the victory parade, the days
of celebrating annexation. I've seen lightning flashes,
driving rain. When something inside me explodes
like a heart valve or a vessel going under a bridge
yes then, finally, politicians also feel my pain.

THURSDAY 19 JANUARY (DAY 330)
Missile systems designed to intercept aircraft and incoming missiles appear to have
been deployed on the rooftops of several defence and administrative buildings in
downtown Moscow, signalling that the Kremlin is preparing to defend itself from a
potential attack. Photographs published on social media showed a Pantsir missile
system had been installed on the roof of an eight-storey building used by the Russian
defence ministry next to the Moskva River. Another video showed the air defence
system being lifted on to the roof of an education building in Moscow's Taganka
district, 1.5 miles south-east of the Kremlin.

The Counter-Argument

My dearest friend, come to your sense!
You've been tricked! Their goal is to rid the country
of its inhabitants, and clear the way for mining!

Don't trust the Western narrative! Just take a step
backwards and take a good look at the 'agreements'
between the West and Russia, now disregarded.

Nothing is quite as simplistic as our leaders
would have us believe. As usual, the countries
that earn the most from warmongering

are up front and centre gathering their profits,
fighting as always over assets, not ideals.
The truth is the West wanted this war!

Why else would they test the borders
and disregard the 'accords' made with Russia?
It's clearly a deliberate attempt by the West

to gain control of Ukraine and its assets.
The USA will be the bull looking across the fence
at Russia, so Russia simply can't afford to lose!

EU members immediately offered sanctuary
just to get Ukrainians out of their own country
so that they could start mining straight away!

They might have settled them in their own country!
Blindly people follow the narrative of politicians
and believe that they have their interests at heart.

Ukrainian assets are what the politicians and armies want!
To hell with the people, they are irrelevant! It is sadly,
time and time again, what I have seen in any war.

Don't argue with me! You only show your ignorance!
Ignorance is bliss! Why do you refuse to do any research
and just follow the lead of the media blindly?

Will you only be satisfied when we have a nuclear war? Pointing fingers will not help then! When you are roasted alive you will not be supporting a war in Ukraine then!

Look, you idiot, I have my hand on the button now! See, it's trembling with every new tank you send! What are you going to do? Do you want me to nuke you?

FRIDAY 20 JANUARY (DAY 331)

Today has seen a meeting of defence ministers from 50 countries at Ramstein Air Base in Germany. President Zelenskyy spoke via video link to the meeting and reminded those present that it was in their power to make a decision in principle to send tanks. During the meeting, ministers agreed to provide Kyiv with billions of dollars' worth of military hardware, including armoured vehicles and munitions. Despite Zelenskyy's appeal, however, no decision on tanks was made. After the meeting, responding to a question about tanks, US President Joe Biden told reporters that 'Ukraine is going to get all the help they need.' Commenting on the meeting, a Kremlin spokesperson said that supplying additional tanks to Kyiv would not 'fundamentally change anything' and that the West will 'regret its delusion' that Ukraine could win on the battlefield. British foreign secretary James Cleverly announced that the UK is joining a group of international partners to pursue criminal accountability for Russia's invasion of Ukraine. Russia's 'atrocities must not go unpunished,' Cleverly said in a statement, citing the deaths of soldiers and civilians and the displacement of millions of Ukrainians. In a post on the Telegram social media app, Medvedev directly threatened the West with nuclear strikes if Russia one day loses the Ukraine war. The Biden administration upgraded its classification of Russia's Wagner Group to a 'significant transnational criminal organisation' and announced coming sanctions against the private military group.

The New Now

Places we stopped on the road
for a coffee, a beer,
an ice for the kids.

Favourite times.
Times that lived in our minds.
Times we drove to your parents
stopping en route,
the light through the pines
and a bird we couldn't recognise
that sang just for us.

And, before the kids were born,
other times, other journeys
with other people.
Times we don't talk about,
that we never shared
because that was then
and this is now.

So what is this now? This new now?
Now everything is broken:
the inn, the country station,
the domed church –
all the memories we shared
and the memories we did not share.

Tomorrow, we'll speak about
this new now, as if it still existed.
Even if no bird sings
we won't forget.

SATURDAY 21 JANUARY (DAY 332)
A tearful President Zelenskyy attended a memorial service to commemorate seven
senior interior ministry officials killed in a helicopter crash on Wednesday. The
interior minister Denys Monastyrskyi, his deputy and five others were killed when
their helicopter plummeted amid fog into a nursery on the eastern outskirts of Kyiv.
Including those on the ground, a total of 14 people were killed.

Counting Tanks

The peaceful old men
are counting their tanks
1, 2, 3, 4, 5, 6...

The greedy old men
are counting their tanks
1, 2, 3, 4, 5, 6...

The cowardly old men
are counting their tanks
1, 2, 3, 4, 5, 6...

The rich old men
are counting their tanks
1, 2, 3, 4, 5, 6...

Oh dear, we missed one tank.
We must start all over again.

The peaceful old men
are counting their tanks
1, 2, 3, 4, 5, 6...

SUNDAY 22 JANUARY (DAY 333)

Ukrainians celebrate the Day of the Unity of Ukraine. The war in Ukraine is in a state of deadlock, according to the UK Ministry of Defence. In an intelligence update, it said there was a possibility of Russian advances around the heavily contested city of Bakhmut in the Donbas, but otherwise little movement. An adviser to President Zelenskyy has said that caution and slow decision making over whether to send Leopard 2 tanks to Ukraine is costing lives and has told the West to 'think faster'. Baltic countries have told Germany to send the tanks immediately to Ukraine after perceived heel-dragging by the government in Berlin. Latvia, Estonia and Lithuania all tweeted that tanks are 'needed to stop Russian aggression'. The German defence minister Boris Pistorius said that despite heightened expectations 'we still cannot say when a decision will be taken, and what the decision will be, when it comes to the Leopard tank'. Germany has said it is doing a stocktake of its current tank numbers ahead of a possible decision.

Double Down

Double down on lies
Double down on blame
Double down on compromise
Double down on false claims

Double down on security
Double down on the elite
Double down with new decrees
Double down on the streets

Double down on body doubles
Double down on conspiracies
Double down on the rouble
Double down on brutality

Double down on less candour
Double down on nuclear threats
Double down on propaganda
Double down on whatever shit comes next

Double down with your foot to the floor
Double down past the off-ramps
Double down like your life depended on this war
Double down – then vamp

MONDAY 23 JANUARY (DAY 334)
Russia is downgrading diplomatic relations with NATO member Estonia, accusing Tallinn of 'total Russophobia'. Latvia will downgrade its diplomatic ties with Russia and has asked its Russian ambassador to leave the country by 24 February. Former UK Prime Minister Boris Johnson made a surprise visit to Ukraine, where he said that it was 'the moment to double down and to give the Ukrainians all the tools they need to finish the job'. A divisive figure in the UK, Johnson remains popular in Ukraine where he is credited with helping to galvanise Western support for the country. Norway's army chief has estimated 180,000 Russian troops have been killed or wounded over the course of the conflict. Also today, the EU's 27 foreign ministers met in Brussels and agreed a new military aid package to Ukraine worth €500 million.

Death of My Beard

According to the command
I should raze my beard –
every hair on my chin.

I heard a little voice.
It was my beard speaking.
It asked me to spare its life.

Usually my beard
has a reliable, salty character,
but now it seemed afraid.

Ahead of us lay broken ground,
whistling of shells overhead,
dead men in eyesight.

Well, I would find some water,
mix it with soap, and somehow locate
the standard issue blade.

I told my beard, don't be afraid,
Your death is coming fast.
To die for the motherland is an honour.

My beard screamed a lot
as I shaved it off. I can't say
if it died for a good cause or not.

TUESDAY 24 JANUARY (DAY 335)
General Valery Gerasimov, who was appointed war commander for Russian forces
on 11 January, has ordered Russian soldiers to improve their 'day-to-day discipline'
and has clamped down on uniform enforcement, ordering Russian soldiers to stop
wearing non-regulation uniform, travelling in civilian vehicles and using mobile
phones. He has also issued an order banning beards, saying troops must be clean-
shaven on the battlefield, a move that is bound to be unpopular with bearded Chechen
troops. Gerasimov replaced General Sergei Surovikin after only three months in the
role. Surovikin gained his nickname 'General Armageddon' while leading Russian
forces in Syria where he was accused of overseeing a brutal bombardment of Aleppo.

Polite Request to Visitors

Don't steal animals
when you visit the zoo.
Animals belong with
their keepers, not to you.

Please don't break
the enclosure of the lions.
It's for good reason
that it's made of iron.

Don't poke the leopards
asleep in their cage.
No door can hold back
wild things in a rage.

WEDNESDAY 25 JANUARY (DAY 336)

A team at Berlin Zoo has raised €400,000 in contributions from well-wishers to pay for generators and fodder for Kyiv Zoo. During the power cuts created by Russian missile strikes, Kyiv Zoo has been warming the primate enclosure with a wood-fired oven because temperatures of −10°C at night are too cold for the animals. Zoo animals have suffered greatly during the war: many were stolen from Kherson Zoo in November (including a racoon taken by the Russian military as a trophy) and, in March, a young lion escaped when its cage was damaged at Kharkiv Zoo. Today, President Biden approved sending 31 M1 Abrams tanks to Ukraine and Germany also confirmed it will make 14 Leopard 2A6 tanks available for Ukraine's war effort. Germany will also approve other European countries supplying German-made Leopard 2 tanks from their own stock and Finland, Spain and the Netherlands have said they will contribute the same model. A second battalion will be made up of Leopard 2A4 tanks from Poland and Norway. In response to these developments, the secretary of Russia's security council, Nikolai Patrushev, a close ally of Putin, said that the US and NATO were parties to the conflict in Ukraine and were seeking to drag out the fighting.

The Waves

The waves from the Caspian Sea
leave foaming contrails
across the cold blue sky.

Many stutter, are brought down,
but every seventh one
reaches its destined landing point

with a spurt of earth,
a cloud and a hard sonic blast
of dust and metal shards.

The waves from the Caspian Sea
lance blood and soil
as they wash over Ukraine

putting out lights everywhere,
on autoroutes, railway stations,
kitchens and bedrooms.

Televisions blink to blackness,
freezers fail, kettles, ovens die
while the snow drifts outside.

The people of the cities of Ukraine
in darkness everywhere,
wave two fingers at the waves.

In the metro, they talk and sing,
send messages or listen to music
on well-charged phones.

Waiting

They sit in their homes,
waiting for the war to blow over,
flinching with each new grad that lands.

'There was nothing here before.
I built it all with my bare hands.
No one can drive me out of here.'

'Come, we beg you, come now –
the fighting is only a hundred metres away.
You can come back after winter!'

'And what then? Where will I go?
I'll have to beg for bread, cap in hand?
No! I lived this long. I'll continue.'

(*grad*: a Russian artillery shell)

THURSDAY 26 JANUARY (DAY 337)
Today was President Zelenskyy's 45th birthday. Russia launched several volleys of
missiles with strikes reported across the country killing at least 11 people. The wave of
strikes came a day after Germany and the United States pledged to send dozens of
battle tanks to Ukraine, a significant step up in Western military support. Several large
explosions shook Kyiv at about 10 a.m. local time. Ukraine's Air Force command said
that Russia fired 55 missiles at targets across the country and that 47 were shot down.
Ukraine's State Emergency Service said that 11 people were killed in strikes across 11
regions of the country. Another 11 people were wounded in the attacks, which
damaged 35 buildings. A 12th civilian was killed later in the day when a Russian rocket
hit a village council building in Kochebeivka, a tiny community in the Kherson region.
The head of the International Atomic Energy Agency, Rafael Grossi, who visited
Ukraine last week, said IAEA monitors reported powerful explosions near Ukraine's
Russian-occupied Zaporizhzhia nuclear power station on Thursday and renewed calls
for a security zone around the plant. Ukraine confirmed that its troops had withdrawn
from the eastern town of Soledar in the Donetsk region which has seen intense fighting
in the past weeks. The town is almost completely flattened. Ukraine continues to
defend the nearby town of Bakhmut despite months of Russian attacks.

Propagandist

In the deep well he drank
a cup of ink, burped
his troll incantations
up the shaft, into the world.

Madmen, dictators, came to wish
but, instead of pennies, hurled
buckets of shit, then cocked their ears
for the noises he'd make,
their propagandist.

FRIDAY 27 JANUARY (DAY 338)
The Kremlin said on Friday that President Joe Biden had the key to end the conflict in Ukraine by directing Kyiv to settle, but that Washington had so far not been willing to use it. 'On the contrary, he [Biden] chooses the path of further pumping weapons into Ukraine,' the Kremlin spokesman said. On Russian TV, Kremlin propagandists have begun discussing the need for Russia to attack NATO. The Ukrainian government is making a crackdown on corruption. More than a dozen officials have been removed this week after a series of scandals and graft allegations. Tass is reporting that the occupied Ukrainian regions of Donetsk, Luhansk, Zaporizhzhia and Kherson are to be ordered to use Moscow time instead of Kyiv time.

Memorial to Dnipro, Moscow

I am the bow
of the old man who stops
at the makeshift memorial to Dnipro.

I am a flower
in the fist of a policeman
lifted from the memorial to Dnipro.

I am a teardrop
in the hood of a coat
of a woman who holds up a sign –
'Ukraine is not our enemy, they are our brothers.'

I am a flower, I am a teardrop, I am the bow.
This is what makes me human.

SATURDAY 28 JANUARY (DAY 339)
Two weeks after the missile strike on an apartment building of Dnipro in Ukraine in
which 46 people were killed and 80 injured, a few Muscovites still come to pay their
respects to those who died at the statue of Ukrainian poet Lesya Ukrainka in a suburb
of Moscow. Unofficial memorials also exist in cities around the country. The
memorials are routinely cleared by municipal services but reappear the next day.
President Zelenskyy said that Ukraine will launch an international campaign to keep
Russia out of the 2024 Olympics to be held in Paris, saying that Russia would try to
justify their war against Ukraine if allowed to compete. Ukraine's deputy foreign
minister, Andriy Melnyk, called on Germany to send his country a submarine, saying
'Germany (*ThyssenKrupp*) produces one of the world's best submarines HDW Class
212A. The Bundeswehr has six such U-boats. Why not send one to Ukraine? Then
we'll kick the Russian fleet out of the Black Sea.' Russian construction workers have
started the complete dismantling of the Azovie neighbourhood of Russian-occupied
Mariupol, including undamaged houses, to build 'elite' homes, according to Petro
Andryshchenko, an adviser to the city's mayor. Russia has begun bulldozing
Mariupol's ruined apartment buildings for several months, an operation criticised by
multiple human rights organisations who perceive the work as an attempt to cover up
war crimes.

Extraordinary People

Extraordinary people are dying
as well as ordinary ones,
instinctively planting their bodies
nakedly in the way of destruction.

The strands inside them are coiled
tightly against fear – they may seem
quite ordinary, but the tiniest difference
can turn everything around.

And that's how extraordinary it appears
when, in this vast impromptu of death,
an old lady is collected from hell on earth
in the back of a mud-splashed car.

SUNDAY 29 JANUARY (DAY 340)
It is reported that Kyiv and its Western allies are engaged in 'fast-track' talks on the possibility of equipping Ukraine with long-range missiles and military aircraft. An adviser to President Zelenskyy said Ukraine's supporters in the West 'understand how the war is developing' and the need to supply planes capable of providing cover for the armoured fighting vehicles that the United States and Germany have pledged. Ukraine said on Friday it would take its pilots about six months to train for combat in Western fighter jets such as US F-16s. Russian shelling of residential areas in Ukraine's southern city of Kherson left at least three people dead and ten injured. Russian forces targeted a hospital, school, bus station, post office, bank and residential buildings in a strike on Sunday. Mourners gathered in Kyiv today to commemorate voluntary aid worker Andrew Bagshaw (47) and fellow volunteer Chris Parry (28). Both men were killed during an attempted humanitarian evacuation near Soledar in early January. Several dozen mourners, including fellow volunteers who knew the men, came to express their condolences at a small church on the territory of Kyiv's ancient St Sophia Cathedral. The bodies of both men were returned to Ukraine in early February. Andrew Bagshaw was formerly a University of Otago geneticist who gained his PhD in 2008. He was described by his PhD supervisor as 'a genuine genius, easily one of the most extraordinary students I have trained'. Chris Parry was a running coach from Cornwall.

Measuring the Distance

And that's when the Olympian jumps
and they slow down the film – suddenly
he's leaping not only the sand pit
but also the stadium, also the town,

over fields, farms and even far-off cities.
Cars, buses, trains move on the roads
and rails below him, birds swoop
and catch his eye as he continues on

towards the hazy smoke on the horizon
which, as he nears, becomes resolved
as smouldering towns, fields aflame,
chaos, desecration, desolation…

And that's where the Olympian chances
to fall, in a pit of ashes and dust. The film
speeds up once more – and the judges
are right there with him, measuring the distance.

MONDAY 30 JANUARY (DAY 341)
Washington-based think tank the Institute for the Study of War has said that delay in
the provision of necessary military aid by Western powers has exacerbated 'stalemate'
conditions and limited Ukraine's ability to regain significant portions of territory
through counter-offensive operations. Ukraine's foreign minister Dmytro Kuleba
added to the pressure Ukraine is putting on the International Olympic Committee
(IOC) to ban Russia from the 2024 Olympic Games, saying, 'Russia won 71 medals in
the Tokyo Olympics and 45 of them were won by athletes who are also members of
the Central Sports Club of the Russian Army. The army that commits atrocities, kills,
rapes and loots. This is who the ignorant IOC wants to put under a white flag and
allow to compete.' Ukraine has imposed sanctions against 182 Russian and Belarusian
companies in the latest of a series of steps to block Moscow's and Minsk's connections
to Ukraine. The sanctioned companies chiefly engage in the transportation of goods,
vehicle leasing and chemical production. France and Australia have announced plans
to jointly manufacture ammunition for Ukraine and will make 'several thousands' of
155-millimetre shells with delivery aimed at the first quarter of 2023.

Meat Grinder

It's not one side that grinds
while the other's only meat.

Death visits both side of the street
while his handle each way winds.

The UK has decided to transfer £2.3 billion to Ukraine, money coming from the sale of Chelsea FC after it was sold by a Russian oligarch, Roman Abramovich, when he came under sanctions in 2022. Ukraine's foreign minister Dmytro Kuleba has said Kyiv expects to receive 120 to 140 tanks in a 'first wave' of deliveries from a coalition of 12 countries. President Zelenskyy said today that the situation in Bakhmut and Vuhledar was 'very tough' with both areas and other parts of the Donetsk region 'under constant Russian attacks'. The battle for control of Bakhmut, one of the bloodiest of the Ukraine war to date, is a 'meat grinder', in the words of Yevgeny Prigozhin, the businessman who heads the Russian Wagner Group of mercenaries. NATO chief Jens Stoltenberg and Japan's Premier Fumio Kishida pledged to strengthen ties, saying Russia's invasion of Ukraine and its growing military cooperation with China had created the most tense security environment since the Second World War. US intelligence estimates that 188,000 Russian soldiers have been killed or injured. The last time the Russian Ministry of Defence acknowledged any army casualties was on 21 September when defence minister Sergei Shoigu said that 5,937 Russian soldiers had died.

Spring Clean

Every year, open the windows with a shout
and let what was eating the curtains fly out.

An agency may be needed to hoover up,
behind the sofa, accumulated bucks.

We recommend thorough de-oligarchisation
when rank odours are bothering the nation.

Don't rest on customs in these trying days,
just take a broom and sweep them away.

WEDNESDAY I FEBRUARY (DAY 343)
President Zelenskyy is currently shuffling the ranks of senior government officials and has said that anyone failing to perform according to strict standards would face dismissal. In Ukraine, two high profile anti-corruption raids were carried out on Wednesday morning, targeting oligarch Igor Kolomoisky and former interior minister Arsen Avakov. Government moves against corrupt senior officials and oligarchs are motivated in part by a desire to proceed more rapidly with complex negotiations to secure European Union membership in the context of a forthcoming talks 'summit' with EU officials to take place on Friday. Russian media claimed today that the town of Bakhmut is nearly encircled after being besieged for months, however Ukraine rejects this assertion and says that heavy fighting continues in the area.

Justice

Some say some have their noses
pressed too close to reality, when really
imagination is the thing for art.
So let's just, for a moment, imagine justice

and what a fitting justice might one day
exactly mean for those who deserve it. Let's
talk about the shape of it, the scale of it
and the exact weight of it in the mind.

Let's carefully assemble the evidence
to feed this imagined justice, the tattered jigsaw
of fragments of bone, DNA, specific
metals, chemicals and signed statements.

Now let's imagine the evidence *is* the justice,
partial and cobbled together, but terrific
and terrifying, justice that stretches out forever
and is served for all time, drop by cold drop.

THURSDAY 2 FEBRUARY (DAY 344)
The European Commission President Ursula von der Leyen has announced an international centre for the prosecution of crimes in Ukraine will be set up at The Hague. The centre will coordinate the collection of evidence for war crimes. Shell has prompted anger after annual profits more than doubled to a record of nearly $40bn, boosted by a surge in wholesale gas prices linked to the war in Ukraine. Oleksii Reznikov, Ukraine's defence minister, has said Russia is preparing a major new offensive and warned that it could begin as soon as 24 February. He said Moscow had amassed thousands of troops and could 'try something' to mark the anniversary of the initial invasion last year. The attack would also mark Russia's Defender of the Fatherland Day on 23 February, which celebrates the army. Mr Reznikov said he believed that Moscow had mobilised some 500,000 troops for the potential offensive. Pete Reed, a 34 year old American medic, has been killed while working on the frontlines in Bakhmut, just weeks after arriving in Ukraine. He died while helping evacuate civilians when his vehicle was hit by a missile.

These are the Days

Let me tell you what I have personally seen:
I have seen a blackbird bathing in the garden
and a Russian crawling with wounds.
I have seen my mother burst into tears
recalling how my father told her 'This is farewell.'
O these are the days, yes these are the days
and these are the things I have seen.

Let me tell you what I have personally seen:
a blur of lights in my telephone's camera
and the laughing face of Putin left by a troll
on my *Facebook* page, a report on Bristol
Airport's expansion despite the government's
obligations, O their obligations for net zero
which I don't believe they will achieve.

Let me tell you what I have personally seen:
Friday dustbins blown over in strong winds
and recycling shuffling down the street;
a dog that howls at me from inside his home
and a soft bright halo around the full moon.
O these are the days, yes these are the days
and these are the things I have seen.

FRIDAY 3 FEBRUARY (DAY 345)
Ursula von der Leyen and senior EU officials travelled to Kyiv today for talks,
offering strong support for Ukraine but setting no rigid timelines for its accession to
the bloc. President Zelenskyy had hoped the EU would put Ukraine on a fast track to
membership. The EU has promised a tenth package of sanctions against Russia
covering trade worth €10 billion and focusing on military technology. EU countries
also agreed to set price caps on Russian oil products with effect from Sunday, together
with an EU ban on Russian oil product imports. A senior Russian lieutenant who fled
after serving in Ukraine described how his country's troops tortured prisoners of war
and threatened some with rape. Konstantin Yefremov told *The Guardian*, 'I have
personally seen our troops torture Ukrainian soldiers.'

In Front of Bowl of Soup

Yesterday, two my comrades died
with whom... almost a year...
we were together.

This news came in very mundane style –
a trooper came in the evening
with TVN... with food...

kind of thermos...
pours a soup
and says... they died.

So mundane...
In front of bowl of soup...
Told about the tragedy...

About the emptiness...
About the abyss...
In front of bowl of soup.

TRANSCRIPT OF A SELF-RECORDED VIDEO ON INSTAGRAM BY A UKRAINIAN SOLDIER

Hopes

Last night I spoke with my father
about how he thinks he is dying
and that the world will soon end.

He wonders why he only has one friend
and why we are all so disconnected.
He asks, won't these wars ever end?

Is it worth making ourselves unhappy
about all the things we can't change?
Why waste so much time on worry?

He thinks I'm lucky having poetry
into which I can pour my thoughts –
some kind of escape, through art.

There are no real answers, he says,
nobody is coming up with solutions, only
all these people dying without friends.

None of this sounded much like him.
Lately, a virus has given him a rough ride.
I hope he'll pull through. I hope we all will.

SATURDAY 4 FEBRUARY (DAY 346)
The United States has announced a new military aid package for Ukraine worth
$2.2bn (£1.8bn) which will include precision-guided rockets and HAWK air defence
firing units, as well as other munitions and weapons. Significantly, the package
includes the ground-launched small-diameter bomb (GLSDB) for the first time,
which will double Ukraine's strike range and allow Ukraine's military to attack
targets far behind the Russian frontlines. President Zelenskyy has said Ukraine will
continue to fight for Bakhmut as long as it can, vowing that 'nobody will give away'
the eastern fortress city. The EU will launch a humanitarian de-mining programme
in Ukraine worth €25 million which will be 'crucial to save the lives of civilian
population' according to EU foreign policy chief Josep Borrell.

One of the Herd

What is your crime?
It's not for me to say what my crime is.
Why are you a prisoner?
I'm a prisoner because I was captured in Ukraine.
What is your crime?
I have committed no crime.
You came to Ukraine with an AK to kill Ukrainians. There's no crime?
I came to liberate Luhansk and Donetsk. The people asked for it.
Ukraine could not deal with its own problems?
I was mobilised. You can say that I was one of the herd.
Mobilised in September? Correct?
Yes.
What do you think about Russians attacking Kyiv, Kherson, Kharkiv?
What do you mean?
Are Kyiv, Kherson, Kharkiv in Luhansk and Donetsk?
No. I don't believe what you're saying.
You don't know that Russians sucked dick in Kyiv, Kherson and Kharkiv?
No I don't. That's not a term for war.
Why did they go there?
Maybe they wanted to make a buffer zone, between east and west?
What is your crime?
It's not for me to say what my crime is. I'm just one of the herd

TRANSCRIPT OF AN INTERVIEW WITH A RUSSIAN PRISONER OF WAR BROADCAST BY LVIV MEDIA ON YOUTUBE

SUNDAY 5 FEBRUARY (DAY 347)
President Zelenskyy revoked the citizenship of several former influential politicians. He would not list the names but said they had dual Russian citizenship. According to Ukrainian state media, the list includes several top politicians from the office of Viktor Yanukovych, former President of Ukraine. Yanukovych was a pro-Russian leader of the country from 2010 until he was removed from office in 2014 by a popular uprising. Ukraine has sanctioned hundreds of Russian and Belarusian individuals and firms since the start of the Russian invasion of Ukraine in 2022. Lviv Media, a Ukrainian broadcaster, has begun releasing consensual interviews with Russian prisoners of war on *YouTube* to try and influence Russian popular opinion.

Old Man of the East

Old man of the east makes a lot of gas,
oil flows in his veins and arteries.
His head gets rich, but this golden mask
leaves him blind. Still, he pretends to see.

Old man of the east likes to trick and lie,
especially to fool that other old man
who lives beyond the sea – the one his lovely
neighbour likes to ogle when she can.

He teaches her words she loves: democracy
and freedom, words that cause growls
on her borders and a groping hand easterly...
'Help me! Help me, please!' she howls.

Old man from beyond the sea comes running
with a stick and a drum, he holds her hand.
Old man of the east gets angrier still – he flings
on his trench coat and invades her land.

Old man from beyond the sea turns off the gas,
stops the oil flowing in the tired arteries.
Old man of the east groans inside his gold mask
as the crude in his veins starts to freeze.

Go back to the east, old man, you were never true,
you lied and cheated, you steamed with jealousy.
Resentment and greed are all you ever knew,
go back to your motherland and freeze.

Embargoes

Embargoes on oil and price caps on derivatives and
pressure on margins and reduced production and
pressure on prices and shortage of tankers so...
Where does the oil flow now? Which way and how?

There are cash flow issues and destroyed gas pipelines and
struggling oil fields and lack of investment and
failures to equipment and nobody to fix it so...
Where does the oil flow now? Which way and how?

Oil in the arteries of Russia and gas with nowhere to go and
crude that is stiffening and beginning to freeze and
hands that start shaking and breathing that rasps so...
Where does the oil flow now? What happened to the cash cow?

MONDAY 6 FEBRUARY (DAY 348)

In the early hours of this morning, an earthquake of 7.9 magnitude hit Turkey and
Syria with around 4000 deaths already estimated. By the end of February more than
50,000 had died, Reuters reported. The UN Secretary General António Guterres said
the world risked walking into 'a wider war' over Ukraine. Addressing the UN general
assembly just weeks before the first anniversary of Russia's invasion, Guterres said:
'The prospects for peace keep diminishing. The chances of further escalation and
bloodshed keep growing.' Russia's oil and gas revenues are 46% down compared with
a year ago, the plunge being due to the impact of the price cap on oil exports imposed
by Western allies. The EU-imposed ban on Russian seaborne oil products came into
force today. The EU will also impose a price cap on sales to non-Western countries. A
ban on Russian seaborne crude came into force on 5 December and the extension to oil
products will mean that 70% of Russian energy exports will now be subject to sanction.
Such bans may have a devastating effect on the Russian oil and gas industry since oil
production in arctic regions depends on a constant flow of oil in pipelines that are
susceptible to freezing. Norway agreed to pass a bilateral aid package for Ukraine
worth about $7bn over five years.

Taking Care

Amongst the rubble
shovels swing in the air –
secretly filmed, though they
thought they took care.

TUESDAY 7 FEBRUARY (DAY 349)
Ukraine has released extraordinary video footage that appears to show Russian
fighters dragging their badly wounded commander away from the battlefield, and
then beating him violently with what appear to be shovels. A Ukrainian drone
captured the incident near the eastern city of Bakhmut, where intense fighting has
been raging for months. Ukraine announced that it had withdrawn from its libraries
19 million copies of books that came either from the Soviet era or were in Russian.
After Russia moved to annex Ukraine's Crimean peninsula in 2014, Kyiv increasingly
restricted the use of Russian books. This 'de-russification' process sped up when
Russia invaded the country nearly a year ago. Ukraine's military claimed today that
the last 24 hours were the deadliest of the war for Russian troops. It increased its tally
of Russian military dead by 1,030 overnight to 133,190, the biggest increase in daily
Russian military deaths since the war began last February. Russia has also said it
killed large numbers of Ukrainian troops in recent weeks, claiming it had inflicted
6,500 Ukrainian casualties in the month of January. These figures could not be
independently verified, but the assertion that the fighting was the deadliest so far fits
descriptions from both sides of an escalating campaign of close-contact trench
warfare. Iran and Russia are preparing to build a factory in Russia that could supply
more than 6,000 Iranian-designed drones for the war in Ukraine, according to
reports. *The Wall Street Journal* claimed that the two governments are moving ahead
with plans and that an Iranian delegation went to Russia in January to visit the
planned site.

Churchill's Chair

I said I felt something
when I sat in that chair
but I do not know what.

Now I know what I felt
when I sat in that chair
as all Ukrainians do.

WORDS OF PRESIDENT ZELENSKYY

WEDNESDAY 8 FEBRUARY (DAY 350)

President Zelenskyy visited London where he made a rousing speech to members of the Commons and the Lords at Westminster Hall. The speech included a powerful appeal to the UK to supply Ukraine with fighter jets and Zelenskyy presented Lindsay Hoyle, the Speaker of the Commons, with the helmet of a fighter pilot on which the pilot had written: 'We have freedom. Give us the wings to protect it.' The speech also included a reflection on a previous visit to the UK, before the escalation of the war in February 2022, when Zelenskyy had sat on the chair belonging to Winston Churchill in the war rooms. Hours after the speech, Downing Street announced that Prime Minister Rishi Sunak had asked Ben Wallace, the defence secretary, to investigate which jets the UK might be able to send to Ukraine in the future. Subsequently, however, no jets were offered by the UK to Ukraine as confirmed by an announcement on 18 February that the UK would 'support the donation of jets by other allies'. The Ukrainian leader also had an audience with the King at Buckingham Palace. The UK announced new sanctions targeting people who have helped Vladimir Putin build his personal wealth as well as Putin's alleged former lover Svetlana Krivonogikh, who is now thought to be worth more than $100 million. A team of international investigators closed their research into the MH17 air crash today. They say that there are 'strong indications' that President Putin personally signed off on a decision to supply the missile that downed flight MH17 in 2014. All 283 passengers and 15 crew died in the incident.

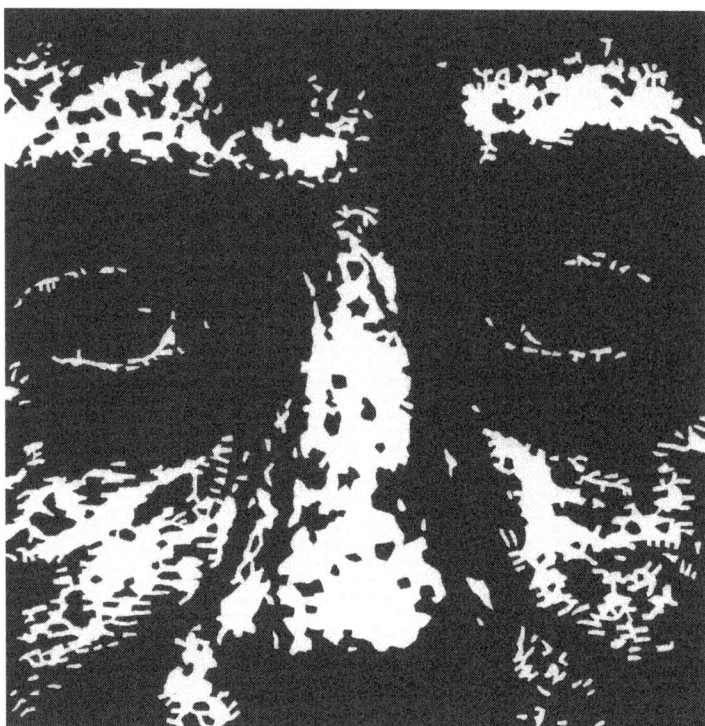

Criminal-elimi-nation

1. Inmates Taken Out

He was clearly someone of importance
if he could offer us a get-out-of-jail pass.
He stood there boldly, like a bolt of chance –
'sentence not important, no questions asked.'
Only six months, he wanted, of our lives,
an opportunity for us, finally, to redeem
our sordid realities, putting to one side
all past wrongs. Was it some kind of dream?

Two hundred signed up. Those six months
would pass in a flash, we thought, after years
of incarceration. In days, we were at the front.
It wasn't at all what we had in mind, our fear
stepped forward now to present itself
and was handed an old gun from a shelf.

2. The Opportunist

At the origin of his death was a con trick played
on the criminal and unwary: that all of this was
so much worse than could have been imagined.

Yet, he saw an opportunity for his own enrichment.
Men died as they were paid to do, he assured it,
and picked out the cash from their pockets.

Not until later did he receive his bullet, dragged
to where a drone recorded, unfaithfully, his death
between cracked walls, by blows of swinging shovels.

3. Coming Home

He wriggled out of the bodybag
cut to his size. Now he's turned the page
and heading away from the frontline,
free as a bird and ready to re-engage.

One day you'll see his face in the street,
the same one you saw on the local news.
Yes, it's him, the one who scared
the old folk, robbed them and abused.

The murderers are coming home –
despite the facts, they managed to survive.
Let go just like that, no psychologist
to inspect their trauma, they just arrive.

So lock the door, keep your kids at home.
Remember, that argument down at the lake?
When he killed his friend with a rock?
Now he's a hero of the state.

THURSDAY 9 FEBRUARY (DAY 351)
President Zelenskyy addressed the European Parliament, saying Ukraine 'will join
the European Union' and thanked the bloc's members for their support during
Russia's invasion. The French President Emmanuel Macron said Paris would
continue efforts to deliver arms to Kyiv and that France was determined to help
Ukraine towards 'victory, peace and Europe'. 'Russia cannot and must not win,' he
said, since 'the future of Europe' was at stake in Ukraine. The German Chancellor
Olaf Scholz said it was clear that Moscow would not win, and assured Ukraine its
future was in the EU, saying Ukraine was part of the 'European family'. 'Putin will
not achieve his goals – not on the battlefield and not through a dictated peace.'
Meanwhile, Russia appears to have launched a major offensive in eastern Ukraine
and is trying to break through defences near the towns of Kreminna, Bakhmut and
Vuhledar. One military blogger said today that 31 Russian tanks had been destroyed
by Ukrainian drones after they were sent in without the cover of artillery. British
Intelligence confirmed the heavy Russian tank losses. The Wagner Group claims it
has stopped recruiting prisoners to fight in Ukraine. Russia has plans, however, to
enact a sweeping parole initiative and intends to mobilise convicts into the official
Russian defence forces at the moment they leave jail.

Flying Over Moldova

I flew over my country
like a missile
looking down on towns
and tiny farms.

A lot of places I knew,
places I'd passed through,
and the people who lived there
that I'd once met.

I felt this ache inside my belly
that I knew was part fear
and part knowledge
of the damage I might cause.

Was I flying to somewhere?
Or trying to escape from somewhere?
I knew, but I wasn't sure.
And so I went out of the door.

Three Years to Dnipro

I don't want to bore you with the maths
but, with the Russian casualty rate today,
if they buried their million dead on the way
to Dnipro, the gravestones would overlap.

FRIDAY 10 FEBRUARY (DAY 352)
Tensions in Moldova have caused Natalia Gavrilița, the Prime Minister, to announce her resignation. Gavrilița has supported Moldova joining the European Union, but not joining NATO. The state of Moldova, a small country situated on the south-west side of Ukraine next to Romania, has been under pressure from various sources during the Russian-Ukraine war. These include the exodus of a large number of Ukrainian refugees into Moldovan territory, the firing of Russian missiles over Moldova from the Black Sea and threatening remarks from Russian Foreign Minister Sergei Lavrov. Some of the missiles traversing Moldovan air space have fallen into Moldova. Ukraine said Russia launched 'massive' missile and drone attacks today, a day after President Zelenskyy visited some European countries to push for long-range weapons. In the morning, Russia struck cities and critical infrastructure facilities, directing more than 100 missiles throughout the country, of which 61 were destroyed. Ukraine also accused Russia of firing two missiles that crossed into Moldovan and Romanian airspace before entering Ukraine. Romania is a NATO member. Ukraine officially asked the Netherlands for F-16 fighter jets today, in order to help defend its airspace. Yevgeny Prigozhin, the head of the Wagner Group of mercenaries, has said it could take two years for Russia to fully control the Donetsk and Luhansk regions in eastern Ukraine, two regions whose capture Moscow has stated as a key goal of the war. 'If we have to get to the Dnipro, then it will take about three years,' Prigozhin added. Meanwhile, Ukrainian troops are still defending the stronghold of Bakhmut which Russia has been trying to capture for many months at huge cost of life.

Labelling

We know what our sphere is
and we dream of extending it.

Are you of their sphere
or of our sphere?

Please, if you are of their sphere
then label yourself as such.

Because we would like, of course,
to be absolutely clear

where our sphere ends
and theirs begins.

And if you can't apply your own label
then we'll need to audit you

and provide you with labels.
Please stick them on yourself.

Now we know to which sphere you belong.
And everyone else can see it too.

You are not us. You are foreign agents.
The label says so. It must be true.

SATURDAY 11 FEBRUARY (DAY 353)
Zemfira, one of Russia's most popular singers, has been placed on a list of 'foreign agents' on the grounds that she supported Ukraine and criticised Russia's 'special military operation' in that country. Activists Aleksandra Kazantseva and Tatyana Nazambaeva have also been placed on the same list for carrying out 'LGBT propaganda'. Many individuals and organisations in Russia have been targeted by measures to label them as representing or being controlled by foreign powers – an attempt to undermine and censor them. The death toll from the devastating earthquake in Turkey and Syria has now passed 28,000. Ukraine has sent 88 rescue experts to help search flattened buildings for survivors, erect tents and offer first aid. The team includes specialists in search and rescue operations, doctors, dog handlers and firefighters.

Day 354

Maryinka stands. Maryinka was destroyed –
not a single building remains.
The landscape of the city is burnt trees
and the remains of houses.

Bakhmut stands. Bakhmut is a shell.
The thud of artillery echoes
through empty streets where missiles
have punched holes through buildings.

Vuhledar stands. Vuhledar's burnt apartments
crouch in piles of debris. Surrounding fields
are sown with the remains of tanks
and the bodies of Russian soldiers.

After overnight battles, exhausted troops
sleep in late - then as midday approaches,
the shelling resumes, the dull rhythm of war.
Once more, they tighten their boots.

SUNDAY 12 FEBRUARY (DAY 354)
According to Ukrainian officials, Russian soldiers are dying in greater numbers in
Ukraine this month than at any time since the first week of the invasion. The
Ukrainian data shows 824 Russian soldiers dying per day in February. Oleksiy
Danilov, secretary of the National Security and Defence Council of Ukraine (NSDC)
said that Russia had renewed its offensive campaign but was experiencing great
difficulties in its push to take the towns of Bakhmut, Vuhledar and Maryinka. The US
confirmed it had shot down three spying balloons in the past week over North
America. The balloons were travelling at high altitude and had different forms. It is
hoped that debris will reveal the purpose and origin of the crafts, which are suspected
to belong to China. One of the balloons was about 60m tall and carrying an airliner-
sized load. The other two objects were smaller and are less well understood.

Snatched

Some kind of dream, a
stupid surrealism,
sitting in a trench

in winter, waiting
to kill invaders, awake
but snatched in a dream.

MONDAY 13 FEBRUARY (DAY 355)
NATO's Secretary General Jens Stoltenberg said that he believes a new Russian offensive has begun in Ukraine and that NATO plans to increase its targets for ammunition stockpiles. Russia may have lost an entire brigade of the elite 155th naval infantry while storming the eastern Ukrainian city of Vuhledar, according to a report. A large number of Russian forces, including command staff, were destroyed near the city of Vuhledar. The US has told its citizens to leave Russia at once due to the war and the risk of arbitrary arrest or harassment by Russian law enforcement agencies. France has also strongly advised its citizens against going to Belarus given the 'new offensive launched by Russia in Ukraine'. Moldova's President, Maia Sandu, accused Russia today of planning to use foreign saboteurs to overthrow her country's government, prevent it from joining the EU and use it in the war against Ukraine. Sandu's comments came after President Zelenskyy said that Ukraine had intercepted plans by Russian secret services for 'the destruction of Moldova'.

Valentine

Mad old Putin's
Valentine cupid came
and shot his arrow
in the heart of Ukraine.

Ukraine turned to Putin
and said, 'Which part
of "I don't love you"
don't you understand?'

TUESDAY 14 FEBRUARY (DAY 356)

The UK announced that Prime Minister Rishi Sunak will lead a one-minute silence at 11 a.m. on 24 February as an expression of solidarity with Ukraine. Ukraine's allies have begun training Ukrainian troops on the Leopard 2 and other modern battle tanks. Germany started training Ukrainian soldiers on the Leopards on Monday at an army base in the northern town of Münster. Ukrainian troops are also being trained by Polish, Canadian and Norwegian instructors at a military base in south-west Poland. After a meeting of Western defence ministers in Brussels today, Ukraine's allies have said that it is unlikely they will be able to supply the number of tanks they previously promised. The German defence minister, Boris Pistorius, said they would not be able reach the size of a battalion. The possible supply of aircraft to Ukraine is also under discussion. Yevgeny Prigozhin, the head of Russia's Wagner Group of mercenaries, has admitted that he founded and financed a company the US has described as a 'Russian troll farm'. Prigozhin's statement outlined his specific links to the Internet Research Agency, a St Petersburg-based company that US intelligence officials say was central to Russian efforts to sway the 2016 US presidential election when Donald Trump took office.

Before the War

Before the war, my childhood
was a kind of paradise.
I know now that I lived in Eden
and the taste of it's still sweet –
those times when I was always free.

I lived according to my needs,
which were few, and was intrigued
by whatever lived under a stone,
down a burrow in the ground
or on the curled leaf of a tree.

I learnt I shouldn't care too much,
and not to trust too much. I learnt
what feelings made me sad.
My parents always loved me
and accepted who I was.

I found that friends were fickle
and a good friend wouldn't laugh
at me. I never travelled on a bus
to a camp in a foreign country
for patriotic re-education.

WEDNESDAY 15 FEBRUARY (DAY 357)
According to a new report published by the Yale Humanitarian Research Lab in the
US, at least 6,000 children from Ukraine have attended Russian 're-education' camps
in the past year, with several hundred held there for weeks or months beyond their
scheduled return date. The report also concludes that Russia has unnecessarily
expedited the adoption and fostering of children from Ukraine in what could
constitute a war crime. Ukraine's defence minister, Oleksii Reznikov, has said that
Zelenskyy has asked him to remain in his current post, after a corruption scandal
beset his ministry and put his role in doubt. Russia's army is estimated to have lost
nearly 40% of its pre-war fleet of tanks after nine months of fighting in Ukraine,
according to a count by the International Institute of Strategic Studies. NATO
announced the creation of a new 'critical undersea infrastructure coordination cell' at
its Brussels headquarters to ensure the protection of vital pipelines and cables.

Like Lemmings

Into the orgy of death, like lemmings,
jogging through no man's land, chewing on
amphetamines, hard to bring down –
in front of their speeding minds a gay
or a Nazi, a mad mercenary, an Uncle Sam,
a satanist, a scientologist or a NATO stooge.
But death, when it comes, has the mud-
splattered face of a Ukrainian.

Professional soldiers, icon painters, menders
of old televisions, petty thieves, failed students
and car mechanics all come to a full stop here –
in bursting balloons of violence, pricked
with loud bangs to deflect attention from an
abstract chaos, kicking at the Kremlin gate.

THURSDAY 16 FEBRUARY (DAY 358)
In the early hours, Russia launched its latest wave of missile strikes on Ukraine.
Thirty-six missiles of various kinds were launched and 16 were shot down by Ukrainian
air defence batteries. Critical infrastructure was damaged in the Lviv region but
fortunately there were no casualties and no major impact on power supply. The
number of missiles used by Russia was significantly lower than earlier in the campaign
of bombardment and it is thought that Russia is starting to run low on missile supplies,
having used up a large amount of its reserves attacking Ukraine over the winter. Russia
continues to introduce large numbers of troops to the battlefield in Ukraine, the US
defence secretary Lloyd Austin has said. Those troops are 'ill-equipped and ill-
trained', and as a result Russian forces are 'incurring a lot of casualties', a situation that
is expected to continue. Israel's foreign minister, Eli Cohen, arrived in Kyiv to meet
President Zelenskyy. It is his first visit to Kyiv since the 2022 invasion. Alexander
Lukashenko, the President of Belarus, has said he would only order his troops to fight
alongside ally Russia if another country launched an attack against Belarus. Zelenskyy
has ruled out giving up any Ukrainian territory in a potential peace deal with Russia.
In an interview with the BBC, Ukraine's leader said that Russia would 'keep coming
back' if land was conceded to them. The UK Labour party leader, Keir Starmer, has
travelled to Kyiv to meet Zelenskyy. Starmer said the UK's position on Ukraine would
remain the same if there was a change of UK government next year.

Armageddon Inc.

We'll provide the digital platform
for you to destabilise your country
and if you happen to feel the need
to call for protests and uprisings
against your own government
then that's perfectly fine with us.

Millions of daily views guaranteed
all thanks to our algorithms.
Never mind where your money
comes from, it's perfectly safe
in our fat wallets, an example
of what we like to call 'balance'.

Our friends the Russians consider
that we're a terrorist organisation –
a bunch of no-good extremists!
Get real with your irony guys,
we're just geeks. Don't expect us
to save y'all from Armageddon.

#Instainfamous

Margarita Simonyan
does things no 'ordinary' Russian can
like posting daily on *Instagram*
despite *Meta*'s 'extremism' ban.

Buns, Flowers et Cetera

Buns, biscuits, children, propaganda
children, cake, music, propaganda, heroes,
cats, heroes, flowers, cheese, seagulls,
children, propaganda, dogs, flowers et cetera.

FRIDAY 17 FEBRUARY (DAY 359)
President Zelenskyy today made the opening address to the Munich Security
Conference. He said that it was obvious that Ukraine would not be the last stop of
Vladimir Putin's invasion and that, while the West was discussing tank supplies to
Ukraine, the Kremlin was thinking about ways to 'strangle' Moldova. The conference
is expected to be attended by about 40 heads of state and government as well as
politicians and security experts from nearly 100 countries. The event is being seen as
a key test of the West's resolve to fight out a grinding, prolonged and expensive war.
French President Emmanuel Macron urged allies to intensify their military support
for Ukraine to help the country carry out a needed counter-offensive against Russia.
Olaf Scholz, Chancellor of Germany, said that allies should deliver battle tanks to
Ukraine now and that Germany would facilitate this decision by providing logistics
and stock replenishment as well as by training Ukrainian soldiers. Despite many
waves of Russian missile attacks, Ukraine's energy grid is working without
consumption restrictions across all of Ukraine, with the exception of Odesa. *Facebook*
allowed exiled Moldovan oligarch Ilan Shor, who has ties to the Kremlin, to run ads
calling for protests and uprisings against Moldova's pro-Western government, even
though he and his political party were on the US sanctions lists. In October 2022, the
Russian authorities added *Meta*, which owns *Facebook* and *Instagram*, to a list of
terrorist and extremist organisations. The two platforms were banned in Russia in
March 2022 for 'Russophobia'. This has not stopped Russia's war propaganda on
Instagram (there is an official Putin account) or prevented TV propagandists such as
Margarita Simonyan from making regular posts on *Instagram*.

System of Beliefs

Lies don't fall out of the sky. Brains don't wash themselves.
There are many tangents along which we can act:
the economic, religious and patriotic are all essential.
If required, we can move onwards to oppression, detainment.

The threat of violence hangs over us like a black cloud.
The cloud emits cries, as of those who are tortured.
The cloud is only in your mind... You see? You don't see?
We can supply a video, then, signed with our special mark.

So don't go spouting poetry in the streets. Who wants
to hear that? Don't go laying flowers on obsolete statues.
Everything can be melted down and eventually reformed
including you, your resistance, the contents of your mind.

*(Artem Kamardin, a poet, was detained, beaten and raped by Russian authorities
for a public reading of anti-war poems next to the Mayakovsky statue in Moscow on
25 September 2022. In November, he was sent to the Serbsky Centre of Forensic Psychiatry
for a month-long mandatory psychiatric assessment. He currently remains in pre-trial
detention.)*

SATURDAY 18 FEBRUARY (DAY 360)
China's senior diplomat Wang Yi announced that China would launch its peace
initiative on the anniversary of the war and has already been consulting Germany,
Italy and France on its proposals. At a meeting on the sidelines of the Munich
conference, Antony Blinken, US secretary of state, warned China of consequences if
it provided material support to Russia's invasion. After a year of war in Ukraine,
China has never condemned Mr Putin nor used the term 'invasion' to describe
the war. UK Prime Minister Rishi Sunak made a call to 'double down' the West's
military support to Ukraine. 'When Putin started this war, he gambled that our
resolve would falter,' he said. 'But we proved him wrong then, and we will prove him
wrong now.' Poland is ready to support Ukraine by supplying MiG jets, provided a
US-lead coalition is formed. According to Ukraine, the number of Russian soldiers
killed since the invasion has reached 142,270. Yesterday, the UK's defence ministry
said up to 60,000 Russian forces may have been killed in just under a year.

The Cigarette

She went out on her balcony
at 1 a.m. for a cigarette.

Just taking a first drag,
flicking the ash,
when, suddenly, a missile
passed her on its red-hot
trajectory down the street.

In a blind panic, she dashed
back inside, threw clothes in a bag
and ran out of her apartment.

'Wait, wait! You can't go!'
called a neighbour. 'It's curfew!'

So, after that, she stayed
in the basement. Time moved on.
Nothing
was
ever
the
same.

SUNDAY 19 FEBRUARY (DAY 361)
The EU's High Representative For Foreign Affairs Josep Borrell said the war could
be over in weeks if the EU cannot increase its supply of ammunition to Ukraine. 'We
are in urgent war mode,' he said. 'This shortage of ammunition has to be solved
quickly.' The Russian artillery shoots about 50,000 shots a day, and Ukraine needs to
be at the same level of capacity. The Ukraine war will have cost the German economy
around €160 billion (£142 billion), or about 4% of its gross domestic output, in lost
value creation by the end of the year according to the German Chambers of Industry
and Commerce. Dutch intelligence agencies MIVD and AIVD warned that 'vital
marine infrastructure' could be vulnerable to sabotage and that Russia is undertaking
'activities that indicate espionage and acts to prepare for disruption and sabotage.'
According to MIVD director Jan Swillens this has been occurring for several months
and a Russian ship had to be escorted away from an offshore wind farm.

No. 1 Liberator

The people of the Donetsk People's Republic
are having hallucinations. They think
they can see Joe Biden in Kyiv.
They rub their eyes – and it really is him.

But where is their No. 1 liberator? Why is he
still sitting at his desk? O mighty Putin,
why have you forsaken us?
They rub their eyes. Still no one…

MONDAY 20 FEBRUARY (DAY 362)
US President Joe Biden visited Kyiv this morning, arriving on a train from Poland. Russian pro-war commentators on Telegram used Biden's visit to Kyiv as an opportunity to launch an attack on Putin for failing to visit the war zone. 'Look, there are two grandpas,' wrote Zastavny, a pro-war Russian blog with more than 110,000 subscribers. 'One of them is old, has all the signs of Alzheimer's, dementia, and night-time bed-wetting, the whole world makes fun of him. The other grandpa looks very good, has a spring in his step, speaks well, thinks clearly, and has the widely accepted reputation of a strong and brave leader. But only one of them has actually visited Kyiv. And the other one didn't even go to Donetsk.' Britain's King Charles has visited Ukrainian troops being trained in Wiltshire, south-west England. He also met instructors from a variety of nations, including New Zealand, Australia, Canada, Lithuania, Norway, Denmark, the Netherlands, Sweden and Finland.

Over the Water, Under the Water

Just as some animals can live
below the surface of the water
a certain part of humanity
can live with lies.

Under the water,
the animals say
how we love it here,
who would want to live in the air?

On the other hand, the humans
who live in truth, wake up
in the morning like
big old grizzly bears.

They go outside
and take a yawn in the open air
saying to themselves,
'I think today I'll catch me a salmon.'

TUESDAY 21 FEBRUARY (DAY 363)
Today Putin gave his state of the nation speech, the first time he has done so since
Russia's wide-scale invasion of Ukraine a year ago. During his speech, Putin blamed
the West for starting the war in Ukraine and claimed Russia responded with force 'in
order to stop it'. The speech combined many tropes of Russian propaganda against
the West including saying that in the West 'abuse of children and paedophilia is a
normal thing'. Samantha de Bendern, an associate fellow in the Russia and Eurasia
Programme at Chatham House, writing about Putin's speech in *The Guardian*
commented: 'There was perhaps only one truth spoken during Vladimir Putin's two-
hour state of the nation address: that Russia would suspend its participation in the
New Start [nuclear weapons] treaty with the US. The rest was yet another trip down
the rabbit hole into the Russian President's parallel universe.' At the same time that
Putin's falsehoods were being aired, Russian forces continued to heavily bomb the
city of Kherson, an activity they have been pursuing ever since they withdrew across
the Dnipro River in November. Residential areas, a high-rise building and a public
transport stop were hit with six Ukrainian civilian deaths and twelve people injured.

A Wider War

Nobody flies into Kyiv these days
so the US President takes the train.
A small boy watches from his window
the glinting motorcade that winds
from station to palace grounds.

It's a long way to come to intervene
but not further than the top diplomat
must fly from China, to arrive next day
on Moscow's welcome mat – happy
to pledge his strategic cooperation.

The small boy will grow up some day
in a nation of solders. He'll remember
the motorcade, if not the accords,
when important men came from far away
to push the buttons of a wider war.

WEDNESDAY 22 FEBRUARY (DAY 364)
China's top diplomat, Wang Yi, has met Vladimir Putin in Moscow, as China and
Russia reaffirmed their close bilateral relationship just days before the first anniversary
of the start of the Ukraine war. In brief televised remarks, Wang said China and
Russia were ready to deepen their strategic cooperation. Putin said that 'Russian-
Chinese relations were proceeding as planned' and talked of reaching 'new
milestones' in areas such as bilateral trade. Putin said the two countries had 'ongoing
cooperation' in international affairs and expressed Russia's gratitude to China. Xi
Jinping, China's President, is expected to visit Putin in Russia in the coming months,
although an exact date has not been announced. A group of 10 EU member states has
called for stronger action to stop Russia sourcing military parts through front
companies in neighbouring countries and evading Western sanctions. Pope Francis
today called for a ceasefire and peace negotiations, saying no victory could be 'built
on ruins'. NATO must 'seriously plan' for the likely future reality of a Russian-
controlled Belarus, the US-based think tank the Institute for the Study of War has
warned.

Hedgehogs

Hedgehogs have a rounded body covered in short, dark, yellow-tipped spines. Although their eyesight is poor, hedgehogs have good hearing and a well-developed sense of smell. They are good runners, proficient climbers and can even swim. If attacked, hedgehogs roll into a tight ball so that only their spines are exposed.

Some 7,000 spines cover a hedgehog's body which can be raised when the hedgehog feels threatened. Each spine lasts about a year before it drops out, to be replaced by a shiny new one. Hedgehogs have an intriguing habit of chewing and licking certain toxic substances such as poisonous plants, toad skin or faecal matter. This makes a frothy saliva which they then spread over their spines as a form of additional protection.

Without spines, hedgehogs won't last long in the wild, being an easy catch for predators. Occasionally, it can happen that a hedgehog may lose its spines due to stress-related alopecia. In this case, the hedgehog can benefit from humane protection until the spines regrow.

THURSDAY 23 FEBRUARY (DAY 365)

The German foreign minister, Annalena Baerbock, clashed with Chinese diplomats on Thursday, passionately rejecting their claim that the West was adding fuel to the fire by arming Ukraine. Baerbock said it was time for China to tell Russia to stop its aggression. The deputy Chinese envoy to the UN, Dai Bing, insisted the West was worsening the situation by arming Ukraine, saying: 'Adding fuel to the fire will only exacerbate tensions'. His remarks provoked Baerbock into a powerful rebuttal rejecting his claim that the West was indulging in military spending at the expense of other priorities more important to ordinary people. She asked: 'Why on earth would we do that?' and added: 'We did not want this war. We did not choose this war.' She said her government 'would much rather focus every bit of our energy and money in fixing our schools, in fighting the climate crisis and strengthening social justice,' adding: 'The truth is that if Russia stops fighting, the war will end. If Ukraine stops this fighting, Ukraine ends.'

CODA

This book closes on Thursday 23 February 2023, Day 365 of the Russian invasion of Ukraine. In the past week, the West has made a strong effort to show its support for Ukraine, culminating with the visit of US President Joe Biden to Kyiv on Monday 20 February. This historic visit passed off without incident, although air-raid sirens were heard as Biden and Zelenskyy walked outside among the buildings of the Ukrainian administration. Soon internet memes began appearing showing Biden posing in front of Kyiv landmarks and eating ice cream. Were the photos real? It didn't matter. The President had certainly stood in Kyiv and shown his commitment in a personal act of bravery.

Other acts of bravery soon hit the news headlines as the second year of war began. The first was the murder, in cold blood, of a Ukrainian prisoner of war, Oleksandr Matsievskyi, who was gunned down seconds after he uttered the words 'Slava Ukraini!' (Glory to Ukraine!) in front of his Russian captors. The phone video of this killing was released onto Russian Telegram channels before being intercepted and relayed to the world. A verifiable war crime, it caused huge disgust around the world and Oleksandr was quickly announced a brave patriot and conferred the title of 'Hero of Ukraine' by President Zelenskyy. Zelenskyy said he was 'A man who will be remembered forever. For his bravery, for his confidence in Ukraine and for his "Glory to Ukraine!"'

A second Ukrainian hero died just a week after the news of Oleksandr's death emerged. He was Dmytro Kotsyubaylo who was conferred the title of 'Hero of Ukraine' last year. Zelenskyy said in tribute to Dmytro: 'He was one of the youngest heroes of Ukraine; one of those whose personal history, character and courage forever became the history, character and courage of Ukraine.' Kotsyubaylo, callsign 'Da Vinci', was only 27 years old and had become well known in Ukraine for his seven-year-long service in the war against Russia. Posthumously, he was awarded the Cross of Military Merit.

A third hero is not Ukrainian, but the Russian opposition politician Alexei Navalny, who has now been jailed in Russia for 788 days since his return to Moscow from Germany where he was recovering from Novichok poisoning. The film made of these events, *Navalny*, has in the last few days been awarded both a BAFTA award and an Oscar for best documentary, giving further international coverage to his plight. The film clearly exposes the criminal way Putin has attacked his political opposition in Russia by poisoning and shooting them in order to stifle democracy, debate and dissent in the country and cement his own future as President. While Navalny is not greatly liked in some quarters of Ukraine, he remains an important symbol of the potential for rebellion within Russia.

Today, the battle for Bakhmut continues despite the numerous claims of Russia that the city has been captured, and the fact that Russia has a near stranglehold around the city. The battle has now continued for almost eight months and the city has been the scene of thousands and thousands of Russian and Ukrainian deaths. The great majority of casualties have been on the Russian side following wave after wave of suicidal assaults by men who are fearful of being killed by their own side if they turn back.

These soldiers are not the only ones afraid of what will happen if they turn back. The Russian leadership is in a similar situation. Having launched into a war that they seem unable to win, Russia is now having to perpetuate a stalemate situation. Further mass mobilisation is expected in April which will simply serve to prolong the war indefinitely. However, time may be running out for Russia from an economic standpoint. Although its economy is noted as robust by the World Bank and IMF, the statistics on which this view is based are 'invented numbers' according to Prof Sonnenfeld of Yale School of Management who also says that 'the Russian economy is in a tailspin'. Sanctions on Russian oil mean that Russia has to sell to India and other countries at a markdown that has slashed revenues. In a further blow, the International Criminal Court has issued an arrest warrant for Putin and children's rights commissioner Maria Lvova-Belova for 'unlawful deportation' of Ukrainian children to Russia. Last month, the Yale Humanitarian Research Lab published a report alleging that at least 6,000 children from Ukraine had been sent to Russian 're-education' camps in the past year.

What cannot be doubted after a year of war (still known in Russia as a 'Special Military Operation') is that Ukraine has won the admiration of the world for its defence of its own sovereignty. The military support coming from the US, Europe, UK and elsewhere is the validation of that admiration, and of respect for Ukraine's determination to fight against Russia's invasion. Since last February, NATO Allies have delivered more than €150 billion of support, including €65 billion of military aid. Combined with the effect of stringent sanctions against Russia and an increasing awareness within Russia of how things are going wrong, this suggests that Ukraine may have won the upper hand in whatever comes next.

17 March 2023

Too Horrible to Watch

i.m. Oleksandr Matsievskyi, 163rd Battalion, 119th Brigade

Video will be shown in ten seconds.

Disclaimer: this video shows violence and death.
Disclaimer: you will never forget this video.
Disclaimer: you will probably regret watching this.
Disclaimer: you will carry this to the end of your days.

Swipe right to break the sequence.
Swipe right, we said.
You're going to watch it, aren't you?

'Slava Ukraini!'

(He never liked us to say goodbye. When he left, he crossed himself, crossed the house and himself, and said goodbye to me. He said: 'You look so old, Mum.' And I said, 'That, my son, is having such a hard time, from being so worried.' And he replied: 'Mum, thank you for life.')

Special Military Operation

Putin pretends he's not at war
so that no one can sue for peace.
He performs his massacre unruffled
right down to the last man and beast.

In SHIZO

Meanwhile, starving Navalny sits
in SHIZO. While loudspeakers
punish his ears with the 'wit'
of Putin, he baits his keepers.

(SHIZO: punishment cell)

Cargo 200

a final journey
return of the son
he's Cargo 200
his race is run

the case is closed
his casket's zinc
a photo's hung
the forms are inked

best not see him
truth can hurt
life gone forever
a handful of dirt

into the ground
his sister weeps
his father rages
darkness creeps

ACKNOWLEDGEMENTS

Thanks are due to *The Guardian* and the BBC from which most of the reporting and information in this book have been referenced. Nearly all of the poems were posted onto *Instagram* on a daily basis during the twelfth month of Russia's invasion of Ukraine. Thank you to my *Instagram* followers for their support and comments and thank you also to all the people who have purchased the first two books in this series and thereby contributed to helping Ukrainian refugees.

The poems 'In the Yellow Kitchen', 'Putin Save Us', 'Propagandist', 'Meat Grinder', 'These are the Days' and 'Three Years to Dnipro' will be published in *The Songs Don't Sing Themselves*, the 2023 Poetry ID Anthology.

Nick Wonham's linocut illustrations are based on photographs of the conflict in Ukraine. We acknowledge the photographers from whose pictures these prints have been adapted:

SERHII KOROVAINYI (facing p. 1) The destroyed and uninhabited village of Bohorodychne in February 2023. This village was liberated by the Armed Forces of Ukraine on 11 September, 2022

YEVHENII ZAVHORODNII (p. 10) Firefighters conduct search and rescue operations amid the rubble at an apartment block in Dnipro that was hit by a Russian missile on 14 January. The official death toll when operations ceased was 46, but 11 people remained missing

JAN GRARUP (p. 22) A man collects water from a puddle in a crater, Bakhmut, 24 December 2022

MINISTRY OF DEFENCE OF UKRAINE VIA TWITTER (p. 32) Destroyed trees in No Man's Land at the Battle of Bakhmut

KOSTIANTYN LIBEROV, ALSO KNOWN AS LIBKOS (p. 40) Mud-splattered soldier of the 49th Rifle Battalion of the Armed Forces of Ukraine 'Karpatska Sich' defending the eastern frontier

DANIEL BEREHULAK (p. 60) Oleksandr, 37, says goodbye to his wife Yana, 31, and daughter Ivanna, 5. Oleksandr's family came to spend 10 days with him in Kramatorsk. Today, 12 March 2023, he's returning to a border guard unit that is fighting inside Bakhmut

BIOGRAPHICAL NOTE

Jonathan and Nick Wonham are brothers born in the 1960s. They grew up in the UK during the Cold War period. Unusually for British children, they went with their parents on holiday to several communist countries: Bulgaria, Romania and Yugoslavia. In the late 1980s they visited Moscow and Leningrad during the period of perestroika and subsequently witnessed the falling apart of the Soviet empire. In 1989, Jonathan visited the poet George Szirtes in Budapest and, in 1990, he made a trip to East Germany to see the destroyed Berlin Wall.

During the early 1990s, both brothers visited Prague and Jonathan stayed with Czech friends while visiting different parts of the country. All of these visits impressed on them both the unfairness and lack of freedom under communist rule, a system designed to benefit only the autocratic communist leaders and their close supporters. After many years of living with the Soviet threat, it was a great relief to them both when the Cold War ended and Russia relinquished its grip on many states that were previously behind the Iron Curtain.

Jonathan and Nick have previously collaborated on a book called *Steel Horizon* about life on a North Sea oil rig (published in 2013 by Incline Press as a fine press limited-edition book). They have also collaborated on the production of pamphlets of poetry and prints. Nick is the author of illustrated books published by Incline Press: *Aesop's Fable of the Miller, His Son and their Ass* and *The Charm of Magpies*. His linocut prints have also been published in books and as cards. Jonathan's poetry has appeared in anthologies and magazines as well as in his prose poem collections *Ordinary Others* and *Vulgar Variants*, published by Drizzle-Dazzle with illustrations by Suzanne Smith.

The first two titles in this series of three books following the events of the Russian invasion of Ukraine are *The Lady on the Plank* and *Until Independence Day*, both published by Drizzle-Dazzle in 2022.

COMMENTS ABOUT
THE LADY ON THE PLANK

A brilliantly urgent and generous response from a highly talented pair.

*

A superb creation – very moving and very informative too.

*

A brilliant record of the first 39 days of the war in Ukraine
by brothers Jonathan and Nick Wonham. It's an excellent read.

*

An important and angry response to the inhumanity and barbarism
at the heart of the Russian invasion of Ukraine.

*

I cannot read more than just a few pages at a time
because it is so moving.

*

The strong linocut illustrations are up to Nick's usual
excellent standards.

*

Beautifully put together.

*

It is brilliant… moving and evocative. Nick's prints add yet another
dimension to the pathos contained within the poems. Here is something
meaningful and good from such a dreadful situation.

Sales of *The Lady on the Plank: Poems for Ukraine* raised
a total of £1,356 for Ukrainian refugee charities.

COMMENTS ABOUT
UNTIL INDEPENDENCE DAY

A beautiful book. Poems filled with pathos, clear and accessible.
The events of the day are laid out below each short poem and make
uncomfortable reading.

✻

Excellent.

✻

A fabulous achievement.

✻

Moving and indeed disturbing poems… It was worth the wait.

✻

You cannot read these poems without crying for two countries.

✻

A passionate artistic attempt to put into words and pictures a war that is
so brutal it feels beyond our imagination. The horrors, human cost and
insanity are here on each page. Some books have to exist and this is most
definitely one of those.

✻

Superb

✻

Your book is something special.
Thank you for raising funds in support of Ukraine.

Sales of *Until Independence Day: More Poems for Ukraine*
raised a total of £1,442 for Ukrainian refugee charities.